For the Graduate

Words of Wisdom for the Graduate

Words of Wisdom for the Graduate

Words of Wisdom for the Graduate

Words of Wisdom for the Graduate

Words of Wisdom for the Graduate

Words of Wisdom for the Graduate

Words of Wisdom for the Graduate

Words of Wisdom for the Graduate

Words of Wisdom for the Graduate

Words of Wisdom for the Graduate

Words of Wisdom for the Graduate

Words of Wisdom for the Graduate

Words of Wisdom for the Graduate

Words of Wisdom for the Graduate

Words of Wisdom for the Graduate

Words of Wisdom for the Graduate

Words of Wisdom for the Graduate

Words of Wisdom for the Graduate

Words of Wisdom for the Graduate

Words of Wisdom for the Graduate

Words of Wisdom for the Graduate

Words of Wisdom for the Graduate

Words of Wisdom for the Graduate

Words of Wisdom for the Graduate

Words of Wisdom for the Graduate

Words of Wisdom for the Graduate

Words of Wisdom for the Graduate

Words of Wisdom for the Graduate

Words of Wisdom for the Graduate

Words of Wisdom for the Graduate

Words of Wisdom for the Graduate

Words of Wisdom for the Graduate

Words of Wisdom for the Graduate

Words of Wisdom for the Graduate

Words of Wisdom for the Graduate

Words of Wisdom for the Graduate

Words of Wisdom for the Graduate

Words of Wisdom for the Graduate

Words of Wisdom for the Graduate

Words of Wisdom for the Graduate

Words of Wisdom for the Graduate

Words of Wisdom for the Graduate

Words of Wisdom for the Graduate

Words of Wisdom for the Graduate

Words of Wisdom for the Graduate

Words of Wisdom for the Graduate

Words of Wisdom for the Graduate

Words of Wisdom for the Graduate

Words of Wisdom for the Graduate

Words of Wisdom for the Graduate

Words of Wisdom for the Graduate

Words of Wisdom for the Graduate

Words of Wisdom for the Graduate

Words of Wisdom for the Graduate

Words of Wisdom for the Graduate

Words of Wisdom for the Graduate

Words of Wisdom for the Graduate

Words of Wisdom for the Graduate

Words of Wisdom for the Graduate

Words of Wisdom for the Graduate

Words of Wisdom for the Graduate

Words of Wisdom for the Graduate

Words of Wisdom for the Graduate

Words of Wisdom for the Graduate

Words of Wisdom for the Graduate

Words of Wisdom for the Graduate

Words of Wisdom for the Graduate

Words of Wisdom for the Graduate

Words of Wisdom for the Graduate

Words of Wisdom for the Graduate

Words of Wisdom for the Graduate

Words of Wisdom for the Graduate

Words of Wisdom for the Graduate

Words of Wisdom for the Graduate

Words of Wisdom for the Graduate

Words of Wisdom for the Graduate

Words of Wisdom for the Graduate

Words of Wisdom for the Graduate

Words of Wisdom for the Graduate

Words of Wisdom for the Graduate

Words of Wisdom for the Graduate

Words of Wisdom for the Graduate

Words of Wisdom for the Graduate

Words of Wisdom for the Graduate

Words of Wisdom for the Graduate

Words of Wisdom for the Graduate

Words of Wisdom for the Graduate

Words of Wisdom for the Graduate

Words of Wisdom for the Graduate

Words of Wisdom for the Graduate

Words of Wisdom for the Graduate

Words of Wisdom for the Graduate

Words of Wisdom for the Graduate

Words of Wisdom for the Graduate

Words of Wisdom for the Graduate

Words of Wisdom for the Graduate

Words of Wisdom for the Graduate

Words of Wisdom for the Graduate

Words of Wisdom for the Graduate

Words of Wisdom for the Graduate

Words of Wisdom for the Graduate

Words of Wisdom for the Graduate

Words of Wisdom for the Graduate

Words of Wisdom for the Graduate

Words of Wisdom for the Graduate

Words of Wisdom for the Graduate

Words of Wisdom for the Graduate

Words of Wisdom for the Graduate

Words of Wisdom for the Graduate

Words of Wisdom for the Graduate

Words of Wisdom for the Graduate

Words of Wisdom for the Graduate

Words of Wisdom for the Graduate

Words of Wisdom for the Graduate

Words of Wisdom for the Graduate

Words of Wisdom for the Graduate

Words of Wisdom for the Graduate

Words of Wisdom for the Graduate

Words of Wisdom for the Graduate

Words of Wisdom for the Graduate

Words of Wisdom for the Graduate

Words of Wisdom for the Graduate

Words of Wisdom for the Graduate

Words of Wisdom for the Graduate

Words of Wisdom for the Graduate

Words of Wisdom for the Graduate

Made in United States
North Haven, CT
08 July 2023